WELCOME TO

A TASTE OF
CORNWALL

We hope you enjoy this exciting book which has brought together recipes from all parts of Cornwall, including many from schools and pupils. We are proud to have helped CHICKS bring it all together. The quality of the recipes is testimony to the creativity and quality of our local food. At Ginsters we understand this and today we buy most of our raw materials locally including vegetables, beef and pork, dairy and even flour from a network of local farmers.

The book has been produced to raise money for CHICKS (Country Holidays for Inner City Kids). We have supported CHICKS for over 10 years and understand clearly the invaluable role they offer in providing respite holidays and support to some of the most needy children in the country. All profits will go directly to CHICKS.

So we hope you enjoy the book and the recipes.

Mark Duddridge
Managing Director,
Ginsters, Callington, Cornwall

GINSTERS
of Cornwall

real honest food™

Published by Ginsters Ltd   Designed by Bluestone360   Printed in Cornwall by Brewers, a division of Martin Luck
(CHICKS is a Registered Charity in England & Wales 1080953 and Scotland SCO40536).

We asked some Cornish schools to take part in bringing old recipes and favourite food together for this book and we give special mention to Mevagissey School, Halwin Primary School and St Ives School.

We would like to thank the schools and the pupils for taking part and for arranging the school photographs.

CONTENTS

CORNISH SEAFOOD CHOWDER

50g / 2oz butter
450g / 1lb skinless boneless fish, cut into chunks -
I make this up with three different fish: 1) salmon, 2) a firm
white fish like haddock or cod and 3) scallops or monkfish.
1lb potatoes cut into 1 inch cubes
Salt
Pepper
½ lemon
1 medium onion
4-5 strands of saffron (optional)
560ml / 1 pint of fish stock or chicken stock
2 tbsp double cream (optional)

Squeeze lemon on the fish and season with salt and pepper. Melt the butter in a large heavy bottom saucepan. Sauté onions on low heat until transparent. Stir in potatoes and cook for a couple of minutes, turning the heat up. Stir in saffron. Add stock and bring to the boil. Simmer for 10 mins until the potatoes are cooked. Turn the heat down. Add the scallops or monkfish laying them on top of the liquid without stirring them in.

Steam for 3 mins with the lid on the saucepan. Add the salmon and the whitefish. Steam until cooked about 5 - 6 mins. Be careful not to overcook. Stir the dish gently adding the cream if you wish, but take care not to break up the chunks of fish. Serve with slices of leopard loaf.

Entry by Jenny Agutter, Actress

'This is a dish I love to make when I am at home in Cornwall. Using delicious locally caught fresh fish, nice Cornish potatoes, and saffron a spice much enjoyed south of the Tamar.'

Did you know, over 500 men in Newlyn work in the fishing industry?

CRAB SOUP

1.2ltr / 2 pints chicken stock (we use cubes)
900ml / ½ pints full cream milk
225g / 8oz crab meat
(fresh preferred but you can use frozen)
50g / 2oz butter
150ml / ¼ pint double cream
50g / 20oz plain flour
2 tbsp sherry (optional)
¼ tsp grated nutmeg
Salt and white pepper

Separate the white and dark crab meat. Melt the butter in a saucepan, stir in the flour and allow to cook for a few mins. Add the milk, stirring well and also add the chicken stock.

Then add the dark crab meat, nutmeg and season to taste. Simmer gently for 12 - 15 mins. Add the white crab meat and sherry. Bring to simmer, not boil. Cook for 5 mins and adjust seasoning. Serve with a swirl of cream.

Abbie Trevorrow,
St Ives School

INDIVIDUAL FISH TARTS

For short pastry:
500g self raising flour
125g butter / margarine
Small amount of milk
Topping:
Grated cheese
Breadcrumbs

For filling:
1 small onion
300ml milk
30g butter
30g flour
500g white fish
Salt and pepper

Mix the flour with the butter and bind together with a little milk to make some little short pastry cases (as you would for jam tarts). Blind bake for a short time: 15 mins at 200°C should be enough. Chop the onion and cook in the milk until soft. Melt the butter and stir it into the flour add salt and pepper and then stir in.

Once the filling is thick and creamy add the fish, flaked into small pieces. Fill the now cold tart cases with the filling, sprinkle with the cheese and the breadcrumbs. Bake in hot oven until nicely browned on top.

Best served hot.

Ciaran Careswell – St Ives School

Fishermen will not allow rabbits onto a fishing boat, as it is seen as bad luck.

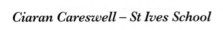

VisitCornwall

Famed for Atlantic washed beaches and scenic countryside, Cornwall is undoubtedly a world-class tourist destination welcoming over 4.5 million visitors each year. To keep Cornwall amongst the tourism hotspots VisitCornwall promotes the county's distinctive qualities to the UK as well as to key international markets.

As Cornwall's official tourist board, VisitCornwall promotes the county as a year-round visitor destination to the domestic market, as well as to key international regions, with the aim to attract new visitors and encourage repeat visits amongst long-lapsed visitors. It seeks to position Cornwall as a world-class, quality destination capitalising on the area's distinctive qualities to broaden and enhance the county's external image.

VisitCornwall also acts as the voice of tourism for Cornwall and seeks to drive up the standard of the tourism product by working with and advising local tourism businesses. In managing a membership scheme VisitCornwall facilitates partnership working within the Cornish tourism industry and offers the trade access to unrivalled marketing opportunities as well as an international platform for promotion. VisitCornwall is part of Cornwall Development Company – the economic development service for Cornwall Council.

Malcolm Bell
(Head of VisitCornwall)

CORNISH POTATO CAKE

450g / 1lb potatoes (peeled)
85g / 3oz beef drippings
2.5 tsp of salt
112g / 4oz flour
85g / 3oz stoned raisins

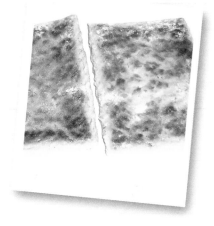

Boil the potatoes with 1 teaspoon of salt until they are cooked. Strain and tip into a cooking bowl. Add 1½ teaspoons of salt and the shredded dripping to the hot potatoes and mash together. Stir in the flour to make a soft dough and add the raisins. Put on a greased baking tray and press out with the hand to about ¼ inch thickness. Baste with milk and bake in a hot oven, 420°F for 20 - 30 mins until nicely browned.

There are thousands of different varieties of potatoes grown around the world, with over 80 on sale in the UK. But China is the world's biggest potato producer.

CORNISH SAFFRON SOUP

2 onions, chopped
2 potatoes, chopped
900ml / 1½ pints milk
¼ tsp saffron infused in a little warm water
Salt and pepper
75g / 3oz Cheddar cheese, grated
30ml / 2 tbsp double cream

Place potatoes and onions in a saucepan with the milk. Bring to boil then simmer for 20 mins. The vegetables should be tender. Blend in a food processor, or use a hand blender and return the mixture to the saucepan and reheat. Add the saffron, season to taste and add the cheese, stirring until melted, stay on a low heat. Remove from the heat and swirl in the cream before serving. You can also sprinkle some grated cheese on top - this gives it a rich aroma.

*Joel Ninnes,
St Ives School*

CORNISH FISH SOUP

1 fresh white fish (haddock
or cod) filleted
149g / ¼ pint of water
560ml / 1 pint of milk
1 large onion small diced
2 chillies

Clove of garlic
Ginger pinch
½ tsp chopped dill to
sprinkle
50g / 2oz Seaweed (optional)

Put the fish and water in a saucepan and boil the fish to shreds, strain off surplus water and add to milk in pan. Finely chop the chillies, garlic, ginger and seaweed (optional to blend). Add onion. Simmer until the onion is cooked, then serve hot with salt and pepper and a little sprinkle of dill.

Louis B Clarke, St Ives School

The colour of a chilli is no indication of its spiciness, but size usually is - the smaller the pepper, the hotter it is.

Hearty Veg & Tomato Soup

½ swede
3 or 4 carrots
1 parsnip
3 medium potatoes
4 or 5 medium tomatoes *or you could use 1 tin of chopped tomatoes*
1 medium onion
Salt and pepper to taste
Generous squeeze of tomato puree
2 veg stock cubes

Chop all veg into good-sized cubes, put the onion, carrot and swede into the pan, add the two stock cubes and cover with water, add a little salt and pepper, and bring to the boil. After 10 mins boiling, add the potato and tomatoes and the puree. Stir in well, top up with water to cover the mix allowing room for it to boil, then simmer for a further 15 mins until the veg is cooked.

Take half the mix out, and into a second pan, and use a blender to form a very smooth paste. Add this back to the pot, stir in well and check salt and pepper for taste.
Adjust the water if you prefer a little more juice. Serves 4, and is perfect for getting the veg into the family, whilst enjoying a great tasting soup. With warm bread this is simply divine.

Cornish Onion Soup

6 good-sized onions
2 medium potatoes
1ltr chicken stock
Small garlic clove
or use garlic powder 1 tsp
Pinch of mixed herbs

Salt and pepper
Fresh bread with grated
Cornish cheddar to top with
Olive oil with small amount
of Cornish butter (50g / 2oz)
for frying

Chunky chop the onions, and fry in olive oil with approx. 50g of butter. Fry them until almost caramelized, then transfer to the pot. Add the chicken stock, and small dice the potato, then add the garlic and herbs. Salt and pepper to taste. Simmer for about 10 - 15 mins.

Use a hand blender to blend the soup, so that you still see some onion pieces, and a small amount of potato. You can thicken if you wish with a little corn flour. Serve with toasted bread and melted cheese on the top. We love to sprinkle cheese just as we serve into the hot soup bowl.

Ginsters employee

The onion is named after a Latin word meaning large pearl.

MARINATED MACKEREL

4 or more mackerel
2 chopped bay leaves
6 cloves
Sprig of parsley
1 onion, chopped
8 - 10 peppercorns
Salt and vinegar

Clean and prepare mackerel and arrange in a pie dish, chop the onion and parsley and sprinkle over the fish. Add other ingredients add salt to taste.

Pour over sufficient vinegar to cover well, add the bay leaves and bake in moderate oven for 40 - 50 mins. When cooked put fish carefully on a dish and strain vinegar over them. Leave until cold and serve.

Halwin School, Porkellis, Helston

LIKKY PIE

225g / 8oz leeks, trimmed, sliced and washed
Salt and pepper
450g / 1lb lean bacon, cut into strips
150ml / ¼ pint fresh Cornish milk
75ml / 3fl oz fresh single cream

2 eggs, lightly beaten
212g / 7½oz packet frozen puff pastry, thawed
1 egg, for brushing on pie top.

Part boil the leeks in salted water for about 5 mins. Drain well. Fill a 1.1 litre (2 pints) pie dish with the leeks and bacon, as layers. Season to taste and pour in the milk. Cover with foil and bake at 200°C/400°F/gas mark 6 for about 1 hour, the milk may look a little strange but that is fine.

Stir the cream into the eggs, and then pour into the dish. Allow the pie to cool. Roll out the pastry, to be a little larger than the dish, then drape the pastry over the top, making a hole in the centre. Well seal the edges, and brush with egg. Bake at 220°C/gas mark 7 for about 25 - 30 mins, until golden brown.

Halwin School, Porkellis, Helston

It has been traditional to serve fish with a slice of lemon since the Middle Ages, when people believed that the fruit's juice would dissolve any bones accidentally swallowed.

MOLLY YOUNG'S SQUID PIE

For the pastry cases :
400g self raising flour
½ tsp salt
3 tbsp olive oil
1 cup cold water

For the pie filling:
1kg squid (850g once cleaned)
Olive oil
2 large chopped onions

1 bay leaf
1 sprig rosemary
6 cloves garlic, chopped
½ tsp black pepper
1 fresh hot chilli, halved and seeded
Sea salt
½ cup pasata and ½ cup of hot water
200ml white wine

For the cases: Place flour and salt in a food processor. Mix oil with water and with motor running drizzle in the liquid. Process until mixture forms a ball. Transfer to floured surface and knead for 2 - 3 mins until dough feels supple and smooth. Put into a bowl, cover and refrigerate for at least an hour. Divide into 8 pieces. Roll each piece thinly on a well-floured surface to a round of about 12-14cm. Fit half the shapes into tartlet tins. For the filling: Slice squid and cut tentacles into pieces 6cm long. Heat ¼ cup of the oil in a large frying-pan (or an casserole with lid) and sauté onion, bay leaf and rosemary until onion is soft. Add garlic and pepper and cook for 5 mins, stirring occasionally. Increase heat and stir in squid. Add chilli and season with salt, then stir for 5 mins before adding the wine and the pasata and water.

Lower heat, cover with a lid and cook for about an hour until squid is tender. Uncover and test squid. The aim is a thick, moist mix without to much liquid. Taste for seasoning. Rough chop the chilli and add back to the mix. Heat oven to 200°C. Transfer mix in batches to food processor and pulse-chop until chunky. Spoon into pastry-lined tartlet tins. Brush inside of pastry edge with water, settle the tops on and seal really well. Make a small slit in each tartlet with a sharp knife. Brush with a lightly beaten egg yolk. Scatter with a few grains of sea salt. Bake for 10 mins and then reduce to 180°C and bake for a further 15 mins or so until pastry is golden. Allow tartlets to cool a little before serving.

Molly Young, St Ives School

RED ROCK COD

6 rock cod
1 carrot, sliced
2 onions, chopped
A bunch of thyme, parsley
& bay leaf

Sauce:
1 tbsp butter
1 tbsp flour
Approx. 315ml of fish stock
Strained juice of 1 lemon
2 egg yolks
Salt and pepper

Clean and wash the fish. Add them to a large saucepan of cold water with the carrot, onions, and herbs. Bring to the boil and simmer gently for half an hour. Take the fish from the liquid, remove the flesh and pile into a dish.

Strain the liquid remaining in the saucepan and reserve for the sauce. Pour the sauce over the fish to serve, you can add green beans to make a real fine meal.

From Ex-pats Peter and Diane Jones Queensland, Australia

St Ives fishermen would not whistle at night and it was a sin to whistle down a mine at night, as it disturbed the mine Knockers (spirits who lived below ground).

Cornish Chicken Pie

3 chicken breasts, skinned
50g / 2oz butter
1 onion, chopped
10g / ½ oz chopped fresh parsley
Pinch of ground nutmeg
140ml / ¼ pint full cream milk
Salt and pepper
340g / ¾ lb puff pastry
1 beaten egg
140ml / ¼ pint Cornish or double cream

Set oven to 220°C/gas mark 7. Grease a 1½ pint pie dish. Cut the chicken breasts into 1 inch pieces and lightly fry in butter until just coloured. Spread the pieces over the base of the pie dish. Lightly fry the onions in the remaining butter to soften, add the parsley, and nutmeg and the milk to bring slowly to the boil. Reduce the heat and simmer for 2 - 3 mins. Pour the milk/onion mixture over the chicken pieces and season well. Roll out the pastry on a floured surface, and cover the pie in the usual way; make a steam hole.

Brush with egg and bake for about 20 mins until golden then remove from oven. Reduce the oven to 180°C or mark 4. Beat the cream with the remaining beaten egg and, using a small funnel, pour into the pie through the steam hole, or carefully lift the edge of the pastry. Shake the pie gently to disperse the mixture. Return to the oven and cook for about a further 15 - 20 mins to ensure the chicken is cooked through. Serve hot with vegetables or cold with salad. Serves 4 - 6.

Ginsters employee

Baked Herrings

8 herrings
Salt (preferably sea salt)
1 tsp ground cloves
1 tsp allspice
2 - 3 shallots, finely chopped
4 bay leaves

Freshly ground black pepper
280ml / ½ pint pale ale
280ml / ½ pint vinegar

Clean and wash the fish. Add them to a large saucepan of cold water with the carrot, onions, and herbs. Bring to the boil and simmer gently for half an hour. Take the fish from the liquid, remove the flesh and pile into a dish.

Strain the liquid remaining in the saucepan and reserve for the sauce. Pour the sauce over the fish to serve, you can add green beans to make a real fine meal.

Ginsters employee

Cornwall has the longest coastline – it's 697km long!

STARGAZY PIE

6 pilchards (or 8 sardines)
225g / 8oz shortcrust pastry
170g / 6oz breadcrumbs
1 tsp ground cloves
1 tsp allspice
Freshly ground black pepper

1 small onion, finely chopped
1 egg, beaten
3 hardboiled eggs, chopped
4 tsp single cream
4 tbsp chopped parsley
Beaten egg for glazing

This is an old favourite from Cornwall, although if served today, we think it might raise a few strange looks, especially from the younger generation… This dish is still served every year at the Ship Inn in Mousehole, where the dish originated from, served on Tom Bawcocks Eve, to celebrate the story of the legendary Mousehole Cat. Set oven to 220°C or mark 7. Gut, clean and bone the fish, cut off the tail fins but leave on the heads. Wash the fish, pat dry, and then open out. Make the stuffing with breadcrumbs, cloves, spice and pepper, mixed with the chopped onions and bound together with beaten egg. Fill the opened fish with stuffing, close up, reshape and leave in a cool place. Grease a 9 - 10 inch flat pie-dish or pie-plate. Spread any remaining stuffing over the dish and arrange the stuffed fish like the spokes of wheel with heads on the rim and tails in the centre. Cover with chopped hard-boiled egg, cream, parsley and pepper; finish covering with the rest of the pastry and pinch the two layers firmly together between the heads but roll back the pastry round the heads to revel their eyes gazing starwards. Brush with beaten egg. Bake for 15 mins, reduce oven to 350°F or mark 4 and continue for a further 20 mins until the pie is golden brown. Serves 6.

James Johnson St Ives School

ROAST SEA BASS

1 large sea bass or 3 fish approx.
1 - 1¼lb each / 500g
85g / 3oz suet
1 tbsp fresh parsley, chopped
112g / 4oz fresh white
breadcrumbs
Sea salt (we recommend Cornish
Sea Salt)

A little milk to mix
Parsley butter
50g / 2oz butter
1 tbsp finely chopped fresh
parsley

Chunky chop the onions, and fry in olive oil with approx. 50g of butter. Fry them until almost caramelized, then transfer to the pot. Add the chicken stock, and small dice the potato, then add the garlic, herbs, salt and pepper to taste. Simmer for about 10 - 15 mins, and then use a hand blender to blend, so that you still see some onion pieces, and a small amount of potato. You can thicken if you wish with a little corn flour.
Serve with toasted bread with melted cheese on the top. We love to sprinkle cheese just as we serve into the hot soup bowl.

Ginsters employee

Mousehole was burnt to the ground in the 1500s, and is now famous for the display of Christmas lights. Coach loads come from far afield to see this spectacular event.

BACON AND EGG PIE

Shortcrust pastry (to line tin and lid):
450g / 16oz self raising flour
225g / 8oz soft margarine
Pinch of salt
Skimmed milk
Filling:
6 rashers back bacon
3 Eggs
140ml / ¼ pint milk
Chopped parsley
Salt and pepper

Line a grease proof pie dish with pastry. To make the shortcrust pastry, add the flour and margarine to a mixing bowl, and rub together until you get a breadcrumb like texture. Add around half a cup of milk, and mix together, until the mix is all collected from the side of the bowl, not to wet or not to dry. Place the pastry in the refrigerator until you are ready to use.

Then lay the bacon pieces in the bottom, sprinkle with parsley. Beat together eggs and mix together, pour over the bacon. Sprinkle with salt and pepper. Cover with pastry to make a lid. Make a small hole in the centre. Bake at 170°C for 45 mins.

Ross Jarvis Aged 9, Delaware School
and Shannon Jarvis Aged 12, Callington College

CHEESE SCONE

450g / 16oz self raising flour
225g / 8oz strong cheese (Davidstow mature cheese)
85g / 3oz margarine
Pinch of salt
2 eggs
280ml / ½ pint milk
Makes 12

Add the flour, margarine and salt together to make a mix. Then mix to a fine breadcrumb consistency, using your hands to mix together. Then add the cheese and mix in again. Put 2 eggs into a jug and top up to half a pint with milk and mix well. Add this to the mix but leave a little egg wash for the tops. Take the mixture and pat it down to above an inch high. Use a cutter and place on a greased tray.

Brush the tops with the egg mix left and cook for 15 mins at gas mark 7 and wait until brown. I remember my family in Cornwall always cooking these scones when ever we visited, and even to this day, the fresh smell from the oven takes me right back to that time.

Mark Duddridge
Managing Director, Ginsters

During a lifetime, the average person eats 35 tonnes of food.

We asked our Brand Development Manager, Graham Cornish (yes that really is his name) to give us a special treat using mackerel, well known for being the fish of Cornwall. Graham gave us two fantastic recipes for you to enjoy...

SOUSED MACKEREL

Clean the fresh mackerel and remove the head and tails. Slice them into large chunks and place in an ovenproof dish. Season with salt, and add crushed allspice [about 6] seeds, 10 peppercorns and two bay leaves. Sprinkle with flour. Add enough malt vinegar and water mixed 50:50 to nearly cover the fish.
Pop into a moderate oven, and bake for 90 mins. Allow to cool in the remaining juice.

SMOKED MACKEREL PATE

1 pack of 454g smoked mackerel fillets
1 lemon (for juice)
4oz unsalted melted butter
3 tsp prepared horseradish sauce
Freshly ground black pepper
4oz of fresh double cream

Melt the butter gently and put in a food blender with the skinned boneless smoked mackerel. Blend to a paste and add to the horseradish cream and seasoning, cut and squeeze the lemon juice, and discard the lemon. Whisk this all together, and hold in the chiller until your ready to use.

Serve with granary toast and a New Jersey royal potato salad with diced red onion and dessert apple, substituting the mayonnaise in the potato salad for French dressing.

Graham Cornish,
Brand Development Manager, Ginsters

Cornwall also tells stories of Pixies, who were very mischievous, and led people the wrong way, and got them lost in fields.

CORNISH UNDER ROAST

900g | 1½lbs chuck beef
170g | 6oz ox kidneys
2 large onions
28g | 1oz plain flour
570ml | 1 pint beef stock
Salt and pepper to taste
10 medium potatoes
43g | 1½oz beef dripping

Dice the beef and kidneys up into ½ inch (12mm) cubes. Peel and slice the onions then place meat and onions in bag with flour and seasoning and now toss. Melt the drippings in frying pan and when hot tip out the contents of the bag and cook to seal in the juices.

Now add stock and allow to simmer slowly. Pour the contents into a roasting tin and add the potatoes which have been halved so that their ends stand up through the gravy. Bake at 35°F or 170°C for about 2 hours until the top of the potatoes brown. Serve with carrots and green beans.

William Facey Aged 9,
Mevagissey Primary School

OYSTER SOUP

2 dozen oysters
110g | 4oz butter (unsalted)
50g | 2oz plain flour
280ml | ½ pint single cream
Salt and ground white pepper to taste
2 egg yolks
Juice of 1 lemon
Cayenne pepper
1.14ltr | 2 pints fish stock

Melt the butter in a heavy bottomed pan. When melted stir in the flour and add the fish stock then bring to the boil stirring all the time. Add most of the cream, retaining a little to mix with the egg yolks, plus the juice from the oysters. Season to taste.

Bring back to the boil, and then strain into a tureen and just before serving add the oysters and the egg yolks which have been whipped with the remaining cream. Stir vigorously. Decorate the top with a dash of cayenne pepper.

Phoebe Hutchinson, St Ives School

The oldest church in Britain is the 6th century
St Pirans near Newquay

THE TRADITIONAL CORNISH PASTY

Pastry:

500g strong bread flour
(It is important to use a
stronger flour than normal as
you need the extra strength in
the gluten to produce strong,
pliable pastry)

120g white shortening
25g cake margarine
5g salt
175g cold water

Mix fat lightly into flour until it resembles breadcrumbs. Add water and beat in a food mixer until pastry clears and becomes elastic. This will take longer than normal pastry but it gives the pastry the strength that is needed to hold the filling and retain a good shape. Leave to rest for 3 hours in a refrigerator - this is a very important stage as it is almost impossible to roll and shape the pastry when fresh.

Filling:

450g good quality beef e.g. skirt
450g potato
250g swede

200g onion
Salt and pepper to taste (2:1 ratio)
Clotted cream or butter (optional)

Chop the above finely then add to the rolled out circles of pastry raw. Layer the vegetables and meat adding plenty of seasoning. Put your dollop of cream or a knob of butter on top. Then bring the pastry around and crimp together. Try practising on a potato first or just flatten like a turnover and mark with a fork. Crimping is the secret to a true Cornish pasty but it really has to be taught as it is almost impossible to describe. Cook at gas mark 6/210°C for approx. 50 mins - 1 hour, fan assisted 165°C approx. 40 mins.

HANDY HINTS

Always use a firm waxy potato such as Maris Piper or Wilja.

Put in plenty of seasoning.

Ensure that all your veg is freshly prepared

Never attempt to add carrot, this is sacrilege!

Use a good cut of BEEF e.g. skirt. This is the underside of the belly of the animal. Its juice produces wonderful gravy, has no fat or gristle and cooks in the same amount of time as the raw vegetables.

Butter or cream gives the pasty that extra richness.

Recipe by kind permission of The Cornish Pasty Association

www.cornishpastyassociation.co.uk

St Austell Brewery Food Champion Paul Drye has kindly selected two special dishes from his range using Tribute, St Austell's flagship ale, as a key ingredient. Paul has a very important role and is responsible for developing dishes and menus to support the breweries pubs making full use of local ingredients. Tribute is the South West's favourite beer and is a wonderful easy drinking ale bringing out the very best that Cornwall has to offer.

STEAK AND OYSTER PUDDING

450g diced Cornish chuck steak
6 fal oysters
1 onion, finely chopped
250ml Tribute Ale
1 tbsp chopped fresh parsley
6 drops of Worcestershire sauce
55g plain flour
Salt and pepper

A little butter

Pastry
450g self raising flour
225g suet
5 - 6 tbsp cold water
Pinch of salt

This classy alternative to the equally delicious Steak and Kidney Pudding uses the best of Cornish produce from land and sea. I have also seen this done with mussels but oysters in my mind can't be beaten!

Start by making the pastry. Sift the flour and salt into a mixing bowl, stir in the suet and then add enough water to form a soft dough, stirring as you go. Place three quarters of the mix on a floured table, dust well with flour and roll out to 1cm/half an inch thickness - large enough to line a 1kg pudding basin. Grease your basin with a little butter and carefully line with the rolled out suet crust pastry. Trim off excess pastry but leave 1cm/half an inch hanging over the edge. Place your shucked oysters in the bottom and sprinkle the parsley over them, then roll your diced beef and onions in the flour and put this on top of the oysters, season with the Worcestershire sauce,

a little salt and pepper and then pour over enough beer to come two thirds up the bowl. Roll out the remaining pastry and place this on the top of your meat, wet around the edge with water and bring the edges together, pressing to form a seal. Cover the top with a disc of greaseproof paper and then tin foil, tie with string around the rim of the basin (if you have a pleat in your greaseproof paper and tin foil this will allow for expansion). Place your pudding in a large saucepan and half fill with water. Bring to the boil and simmer for 4 hours. Keep covered with a tight fitting lid and top up with water during cooking. When cooked, turn out carefully onto a serving dish and cut at the table served with buttery Cornish early potatoes and spring green.

TRIBUTE ALE BREAD

Using Cornish real ale instead of water this produces a wonderfully malty, nutty bread, and the smell when freshly baked is just intoxicating. It's the perfect partner for any home-made soup, but especially a hearty winter broth - this is comfort food at its best.

Dissolve the yeast, malt extract and sugar in the warm beer, put the flour in a mixing bowl with a pinch of salt and make a well in the centre. Pour in the beer mixture and add the melted butter. Flick some of the flour from the edge of the bowl to cover the surface of the liquid. Cover with a tea towel and leave somewhere warm for 10 mins until bubbles start to rise to the surface. Mix well and knead into a smooth dough that's free from stickiness.

You may need to add a little plain flour depending on the strength of the bread flour you are using. When the consistency is right cover again and put somewhere warm to prove. This may take 20-30 mins or until the dough doubles in size. Turn out onto a floured table and knead again - this is called "knocking back". Mould the dough into a perfect ball and put on a greased baking sheet. Cut a cross in the top and lightly dust with plain flour. Leave in a warm place to rise. When the dough has doubled in size, bake in a hot oven 180°C for 15 mins then turn down to 150°C for 5-10 mins. If you tap the bottom of the loaf and it sounds hollow then it should be done. Put on a wire rack to cool before cutting.

STEAMED MUSSELS WITH TOMATO AND TARRAGON

1kg mussels
30ml dry white wine
60g tomatoes, peeled, deseeded and finely chopped
5g French tarragon, finely chopped
30ml extra virgin olive oil
2 cloves garlic, finely chopped
30g unsalted butter

Make sure the mussels are tightly closed. If they are fresh-farmed ones there is no need to wash them, but if they are showing any signs of grit or sand wash them in copious amounts of cold water.

Take a large saucepan, add the olive oil and garlic and soften over a medium heat for about a minute. Add the mussels or pippies, turn up the heat and add the white wine. Put a lid on the pan and cook for a few mins until all the shells have opened, but only just. Stir the shells once or twice during the cooking to distribute them evenly. Remove and pour through a colander set over a bowl.

Keep the mussels warm while you transfer the liquor to a pan, heat until boiling, whisk in the butter then add the tomato and tarragon. Check the seasoning; it's always a good idea to leave seasoning to the end with shellfish because you never know how salty they are going to be, then add salt if necessary and freshly ground black pepper.

Add the mussels back into the pan. Serve with plenty of crusty bread or alternatively with a mound of al dente linguine pasta.

Photograph by
Craig Easton of Driftwood Designs

SALMON PASTA BAKE

Salmon fillets (2)
170g / 6oz of good strong cheddar (grated)
2 dstsp of flour
50g / 2oz butter
Approx. 1 cup of milk
170g / 6oz pasta (preferably shell pasta or penne)
Breadcrumbs (optional)
A little cheese (to be grated on top)
1 clove of garlic (optional) finely chopped, or use ground
Salt and pepper
Sprinkle of black pepper to serve.

Fill a saucepan with boiling water and add pasta, then cook for approximately 8 - 9 mins. Sieve pasta and set aside for later use. Melt the butter in a pan, do not burn, add the flour and still to a tight paste, slowly add the milk and continue to stir, as this thickens, add the grated cheese, cook for approx. 3 - 5 mins until it thickens or until your desired thickness. Fry the garlic with salmon fillets to seal them for about 4 mins.

Place the salmon together with the pasta, cheese sauce, and garlic into an ovenproof dish and grate desired amount of cheese over the top and then sprinkle breadcrumbs. Place in oven and cook for approx. 15 - 25 mins to let the ingredients come together or until it is golden brown on top. Final sprinkle of black pepper as you serve. This is sufficient for two individual pie dishes, and is good served with fresh bread and butter.

Vicky Whiston Aged 14,
St Ives School

CURNOW PIE

8 mackerel from Newlyn
Flaky or shortcrust pastry
3 eggs
1 tbsp tarragon and 50g / 2oz cream
1 tbsp butter
2 tbsp fine breadcrumbs
Salt and pepper
Egg for brushing the pastry

Clean and bone the fish and season with salt and pepper. Butter a pie dish, sprinkle with a thick layer of breadcrumbs and put in the fish, heads and tails off, fully prepared. Beat the eggs with the tarragon and cream and pour into the

pie dish. Cover the dish with pastry, making slits for steam to escape. Put into a very hot oven then reduce, after 10 mins, to moderate and bake until the crust is golden brown. Serve with green vegetables.

Jake Curnow,
St Ives School

The mermaid of Zennor is famous for enticing
Matthew Trewella to his death, with her amazing voice.

We asked our good friends at Duchy College for some of their favourite food. We thank them for the wonderful choice using Cornish ingredients.

ROAST SPICED CAULIFLOWER WITH YOGHURT DRESSING

1 cauliflower, separated into florets
1.5 tsp ground cumin
1.5 tsp ground coriander
½ tsp ground black pepper
Salt
1 tbsp olive oil

For the dressing:
4 tbsp plain yoghurt, creamy if possible
1 tbsp olive oil
1 clove garlic, crushed
Juice of ½ lemon, or more to taste
Salt and pepper
Handful coriander leaves, roughly chopped

Heat oven to 200°C. Boil the cauliflower florets for a couple of mins, so they are not quite raw but not soft. Toss florets in the oil, then combine the spices and salt in a bowl and roll the cauliflower in the mix to coat. Transfer cauliflower to a roasting tray and cook in the oven for 15 - 20 mins or until tender. Allow to cool a little before dressing. Combine all dressing ingredients except the coriander and pour over the cauliflower. Finish with a sprinkling of chopped coriander.

CAULIFLOWER AND CORNISH BLUE SOUP

40g unsalted butter
1 onion, roughly chopped
4 garlic cloves, finely chopped
1 tsp dried oregano
1 large cauliflower, cut into florets
2 tbsp finely chopped flat-leaf parsley
500ml chicken or vegetable stock
150g Cornish Blue cheese, crumbled
150ml milk
2 tbsp double cream
Toast spread with Cornish Blue, to serve

Melt the butter in a heavy-based saucepan, add the onion, garlic, oregano and some salt and pepper, then cook over a medium heat for 5 mins or until the onion is soft. Add the cauliflower and parsley and cook, stirring occasionally, for 10 mins. Add the stock, bring to the boil and simmer for 20 mins or until the cauliflower is tender. Reduce the heat to low, add the Cornish Blue and stir well until combined. Add the milk and heat through gently. Taste and adjust the seasoning. Pour the soup into bowls, top with the cream and serve with Cornish Blue toast on the side.

From Duchy College, Stoke Climsland

Over 25 million cauliflowers are grown in Cornwall each year.

Pork, Cider And Winter Vegetable Casserole

900g diced pork
1 tbsp plain flour
2 cloves of garlic, peeled & chopped
Olive oil
6 shallots, peeled
6 carrots, peeled
3 parsnips, peeled
125g mushrooms
Sprig of rosemary
500ml bottle of Farmhouse Cider (we used
Cornish Orchards, it's just the right taste)
Salt and pepper

Preheat the oven to 180°C. Heat some oil in a sauté pan and fry off the shallots over a high heat until browned, remove with a slotted spoon to the casserole dish and sprinkle over the garlic. Cut the carrots and parsnips into chunky batons. Fry them off with the mushrooms until golden and add them to the pot with the shallots and garlic. Season the diced pork and sprinkle over the flour. Add to the sauté pan, with a little more oil if necessary and brown on all sides (you will have to do this in 2 - 3 batches) and again remove to the casserole. By now the sauté pan will by crusted with cooked flour and caramelised juices - and you don't want to lose any of those colours and flavours. Add the cider to the pan and scrape around with a wooden spatula to incorporate them, then turn up the heat and simmer until the cider is reduced slightly. Pour over the pork and vegetables, add the sprig of rosemary to the pot, pop the lid on and transfer to the oven for 45 - 50 mins or until the meat is tender. Stir once during cooking time to ensure that the flour isn't cooking to the bottom of the casserole, and if there's too much liquid then remove the lid for the final 15 mins of cooking time. Discard the rosemary before serving.

Duchy College Cornwall

Baked Fish With Salsa Verde

Salsa verde:
1 garlic clove, crushed
1 tbsp capers, soaked in water for 20 mins, then
drained and squeezed dry
2 anchovy fillets
A small bunch of flat-leaf parsley
10 mint leaves
1 tsp Dijon mustard
1 tbsp red wine vinegar
Olive oil

Other ingredients:
500g potatoes (any type), peeled but left whole
500g white fish fillets, preferably hake, skinned
and pin-boned
4 tomatoes, thinly sliced
Olive oil for drizzling
2 tbsp freshly grated Parmesan cheese

Place the garlic, capers, anchovies, parsley and mint in a food processor and blend well (or chop finely by hand). Place the mixture in a bowl and add the mustard and vinegar. Drizzle in enough olive oil to give it a thin consistency and season well. Parboil the potatoes for 5 mins, then drain and leave to cool. Slice them thinly. Place the fish in an ovenproof dish just large enough to hold it in a single layer.

Season with salt and pepper, drizzle with 2 tablespoons of the salsa verde, then top with the sliced tomatoes and season again. Arrange the potatoes on top, drizzle with a little olive oil and sprinkle with some pepper and the grated Parmesan. Place in an oven pre-heated to 200°C/gas mark 6 and bake for 10 – 15 mins, until the fish is cooked through and the potatoes are golden brown.

Duchy College, Stoke Climsland

RUNNER BEAN CHUTNEY

1.6kg runner beans, trimmed
1.2kg onions, finely chopped
1 litre malt vinegar
6 tbsp cornflour
2 tbsp mustard powder
2 tbsp ground turmeric
2 tbsp mustard seeds
2 tbsp sesame seeds, lightly toasted in a dry frying pan
400g light soft brown sugar
800g Demerara sugar

Blanch the runner beans in plenty of boiling salted water for 2 mins, and then drain well. Refresh in cold water and drain again. Chop them finely and set aside. Put the onions in a large, heavy-based pan with half the vinegar and simmer for 20 mins, then add the beans. Mix the cornflour, mustard powder, turmeric, mustard seeds and sesame seeds with a little of the remaining vinegar and then stir them into the onion and bean mix. Add the rest of the vinegar and cook gently for 10 mins. Add both the sugars and stir until dissolved. Bring back to the boil, stirring constantly, then reduce the heat and simmer gently for about 1 hour until slightly thickened, stirring frequently to prevent sticking. Transfer to warm sterilised jars, seal and allow maturing for 6 – 8 weeks.

Duchy College, Stoke Climsland

SPINACH OR CHARD GRATIN

300 - 400g spinach / chard
1 egg
200ml double cream
Salt and pepper
Nutmeg, grated
Parmesan, grated

Preheat the oven to 140°C. Wash and prep the spinach by removing any large stalks. Blanch in boiling salted water for 1 min, drain and cool quickly under cool water. Squeeze out excess moisture and chop roughly. Mix the egg with cream and whisk until combined. Season well and add grated nutmeg to taste and a little Parmesan. Season the spinach and add to the cream mix. Combine thoroughly and transfer to a shallow gratin dish. Sprinkle with Parmesan and bake in a medium oven for about 20 - 30 mins until set.

Duchy College, Stoke Climsland

A cat was seen as very unlucky in a tin mine, and no one would work in that section of the mine, until the cat had been removed.

Major International are manufacturers of top quality stock bases, gravies and marinades. Working with our own team of chefs and professionals we use the finest ingredients to ensure we produce stocks "just like chef would make". Our professional stock bases and marinades are available to buy at selected retail outlets and direct at: www.majorint.com

Cornish Orchards produces quality hand-crafted apple juices and ciders using the harvests of small and old orchards throughout the West Country. We started this activity in 1999, as a diversification of Westnorth Manor Farm (part of the Duloe Manor Estate owned and stewarded by the Duchy of Cornwall).

BEEF IN CORNISH CIDER WITH PARSLEY DUMPLINGS

600g lean braising steak – cut into 2.5cm dice
30g seasoned flour
15 - 20g butter, salt free
15 - 20ml oil
150g onions, sliced
20g major beef stock base
380ml water, boiling
250ml Cornish farmhouse cider (We used Cornish Orchards)
100g button mushrooms
150g diced carrots
150g diced swede
100g sliced celery
Dumplings:
35g self raising flour
35g fresh breadcrumbs
20g suet
1 dstsp chopped parsley
½ lemon, lemon rind, finely grated
Salt to taste
Pepper to taste
1 egg, beaten

Serves 4

Toss meat into seasoned flour. Heat butter and oil in pan and quickly brown beef on all sides. Add onions and cook until soft. Pour boiling water over Major Beef stock base and stir well. Add to pan. Add cider. Bring to boil and remove any scum. Add carrots, swede, celery and mushrooms. Reduce heat, cover with a lid and simmer for 2 - 2½ hours or until meat is tender. To make dumplings, put flour, breadcrumbs, suet, parsley and grated lemon rind in a bowl and mix well. Season with salt and pepper. Blend in beaten egg. Use lightly floured hands to shape into 8 dumplings. Place on top of stew for the last 15 mins of cooking time.

Cornish Chicken, Smoked Gammon & Leek Pie

900g Cornish chicken thighs, skinless & boneless
300g smoked gammon steaks (Cornish black pig if available)
225g leeks, cut into 2cm slices
150g onion, finely sliced
¾ tbsp thyme, freshly chopped
1 bayleaf
375ml boiling water
25g Major roast chicken stockbase
225ml Cornish dry white wine
60g butter
70g flour
75ml double cream
Freshly ground black pepper to taste
Salt to taste

Serves 6

Cut the chicken and gammon into bite-size pieces. Put the chicken, gammon, leeks, onion, thyme, bay leaf and wine in to a pan. Pour boiling water over Major roast chicken stock base and mix well. Add to pan and stir well. Bring to the boil then cover with lid and simmer for 30 mins. Mix flour and butter together to form a beurre manie. Slowly mix/whisk in small pieces of beurre manie into chicken mixture and simmer for 2 - 3 mins. Stir in double cream and season to taste. Store and use as required for pies. (Buerre Manie is equal quantities of flour and butter 'kneaded' together).

Drekley is a measure of Cornish time, any thing between an hour and a few weeks

Beef & Betty Pie

700g lean braising steak, diced
40g flour
Pepper to taste
30ml oil
28g butter
375g diced onions
5g garlic puree
300ml boiling water

30g Major roast beef stock base
350ml Betty Stoggs ale
25g wholegrain mustard
150g sliced mushrooms
25g or as required of Cornflour
(mixed with a little cold water)

Serves 6

Toss meat in seasoned flour. Put oil and butter in a pan and heat until hot. Seal beef until brown on all sides, remove and set aside. Add onions and garlic puree to pan and cook on low heat for 5 mins. Return meat to pan. Pour water over Major roast beef stock base and mix well. Add stock, ale, mustard and mushrooms to pan and return to the boil stirring well. Put in covered casserole dish and cook in a pre-heated oven 160°C/gas mark 3 for three hours or until meat is tender. Thicken with corn flour to desired consistency if required. Chill and use as required. Line a pie dish with shortcrust pastry, fill to just below top, add the pie top, remember the breathing hole, and to brush with egg to get a great finish to you pie.

Steak, Mushroom and Cornish Knocker Ale Pie with Suet Crust

350g lean braising steak
15g flour
½ tsp dried mixed herbs
Pinch of English mustard powder
Ground black pepper to taste
8ml oil
5ml Worcestershire sauce
250ml Cornish Knocker Ale
120ml boiling water
15g Major Beef Stock or other

90g small onions
8g butter
60g button mushrooms
Cornflour to mix with a little water

100g Suet crust:
Self raising flour
Suet
¼ tsp dried mixed herbs
¼ tsp English mustard powder

Heat butter in a small pan and brown onions on all sides. Add mushrooms and cook for a further 2 mins. Remove and set aside. Place beef, flour, mustard powder, and pepper in a plastic bag. Shake and mix well to coat the beef. Heat beef in a large pan, and brown beef on all sides. Add water to the beef stock and mix well. Add stock, ale, and Worcestershire sauce to the pan and mix well. Bring to the boil and add to a casserole dish, cover and cook in a pre-heated oven at 160°C/gas mark 3 for 2½ hours. Remove from oven stir in onions and mushrooms and cook for a further 30 mins until meat is tender.

Thicken if needed with a little corn flour mix. Set aside to chill slightly.
Suet crust: Sieve flour into a bowl. Mix in herbs, mustard powder and a pinch of salt. Stir in the suet, and mix with cold water to make a soft dough. Knead until smooth, on a floured surface.
Assembly: Place the cooked fill into a pie dish, and cover with the suet crust. Brush with egg wash and bake in a pre-heated oven at 200°C/gas mark 5 for 45 - 60 mins, until the crust is golden.

Can be served with vegetables in season.

Here at Davidstow it has taken us 60 years of dedication, learning and love to perfect the art of cheese making. It is only when our knowledge, time and skill is coupled with local milk that has been produced by generations of local farmers - that the most intricate recipes can be crafted to create cheddars as special as Davidstow Cornish Classic mature cheddar and Davidstow Cornish Cracker extra mature cheddar. Multi award winning cheddar alive with complexity, buttery smooth character, flinty texture and intense flavour that is far from overpowering, made the way it should be, the Cornish way. You can find more recipes at: www.davidstowchedddar.co.uk

CAULIFLOWER CHEESE WITH SAFFRON AND GREMOLATA CRUMBS

2 small cauliflowers (about 1.5 kg total weight)
1.2ltr full-fat milk
Pinch of saffron
30g butter
30g plain flour
350g Davidstow Cornish Classic Cheddar, grated
2 egg yolks, beaten
For the Gremolata crumbs:
30g unsalted butter
100g fresh white breadcrumbs
Finely grated zest from 1 lemon
2 small garlic cloves, finely chopped
4 tbsp of chopped fresh parsley
Salt and freshly ground black pepper

Serves 4-6

Blanch the cauliflower in a large pan of lightly salted boiling water until just tender. Drain well then place in a large oven proof dish. Preheat oven to 200°C/400°F/gas mark 6. To make the sauce, pour the milk into a large saucepan add the saffron and bring to just below boiling point. Remove from heat and set aside. Melt the butter in a heavy saucepan over a medium heat. Turn down the heat slightly and add the flour then cook, stirring continuously, for 1 - 2 mins, but don't let it brown. Pour in a little of the warm milk and beat to a creamy consistency. Continue gradually adding the milk, a little at a time, beating well after each addition until you have used all the milk up and you have a lovely thick, smooth sauce. Take the pan off the heat, season with salt and pepper and stir in ¾ of the grated cheddar and the egg yolks. Mix well until the cheese has melted. Pour the sauce over the cauliflower in the dish, sprinkle over the remaining cheese and place in the oven for about 35 - 45 mins or until lightly golden and bubbling.

TOMATO AND CLOTTED CREAM MACARONI CHEESE WITH CRISPY PROSCIUTTO

500g Macaroni or 'elbow-shape' pasta
4 tbsp olive oil
2 garlic cloves, peeled and sliced
2 x 400g cans chopped tomatoes
1 tbsp tomato puree
400g clotted cream
350g Davidstow Cornish Crackler Cheddar, grated
6 thin slices of prosciutto pan-fried
Salt and freshly ground black pepper

Cook the macaroni in lightly salted boiling water until 'al dente', drain well, toss with a little oil and place in a large casserole dish. Heat 3 tablespoons of the olive oil in a pan, add the garlic and fry for a minute or two over a medium heat until lightly golden. Add the tinned tomatoes and puree, stir, reduce heat and cook gently for 20 mins or until reduced and thickened. Preheat oven to 200°C/400°F/gas mark 6. Stir in the cream and ¾ of the grated cheddar, season and stir thoroughly into the pasta. Sprinkle with the remaining cheddar and place in oven and bake for 35 - 45 mins or until golden and bubbling. While the macaroni is cooking, heat the remaining oil in a large frying pan and pan fry the prosciutto slices until crispy. Drain on kitchen paper. Serve the macaroni cheese topped with the crispy prosciutto.

CLASSIC CHEDDAR
AND CRAB TART

500g all-butter pastry block, de-frosted
6 free range eggs
600ml double cream
Cornish sea salt and freshly ground black pepper
250g Davidstow Classic Cheddar Cheese,
diced into small cubes
2 tbsp chopped tarragon
2 bunches spring onions, sliced
250g fresh white crab meat
50g fresh brown crab meat

Serves 6 as a starter, 4 for lunch

Preheat the oven to gas mark 7/220°C/425°F. Roll out the pastry on a floured surface to the thickness of a £1 coin and line a 4cm deep, 20cm round loose-bottom flan tin. Line the pastry with a circle of greaseproof paper and baking beans. Chill for 10 mins. Bake in the oven for 15 mins, then remove the paper and baking beans. Brush the inside of the pastry with egg wash and turn the oven down to gas mark 4/180°C/350°F. Mix the eggs and cream together and season. Sprinkle the cheese, tarragon, spring onion and crab over the tart case and pour over the egg mixture. Bake for 25 mins until the custard is set and the pastry is golden brown. When the tart is cool slice and serve with a simple seasonal salad.

CORNISH
CRACKLER RAREBIT

325g Davidstow Crackler Cheddar Cheese, grated
60ml Sharp's Doom Bar Bitter
30g plain flour
25g white breadcrumbs
1 tsp English mustard
3 free range egg yolks
2 thick slices crusty bread
Cornish sea salt and freshly ground black pepper

Put the cheddar and beer in a pan and heat gently until the cheese melts and starts to bubble. Add the flour and cook for a minute then remove from the heat. Add the breadcrumbs, mustard, egg yolks and season. Mix well and allow to cool. Grill the bread on both sides and put on a plate. Top both slices with the Rarebit mixture and place under the grill to brown. Serve immediately. The Cornish Crackler Rarebit mixture can also be used to top a piece of pollock or cod. Bake in a hot oven for 15 - 18 mins and serve with roasted baby vine tomatoes.

KANKER PIE

The meat from two large crabs
2 tbsp of red wine
2 - 3 Artichoke bottoms
3 hard boiled eggs chopped
2oz seedless white grapes
225g / ½lb asparagus
boiled until tender
112g / ¼lb Cornish Clotted Cream

Salt and black pepper
½ tsp cinnamon
¼ tsp ground ginger
50g / 2oz butter
Juice of 1 orange
340g / ¾lb puff pastry

Keep the brown meat and claw meat separately. Mix the brown meat with, cinnamon and ginger then set aside. Butter a pie dish and put in the artichoke bottoms. Next put in the chopped eggs then the spiced brown crab meat. On top of this put the grapes and asparagus tips. Add salt and pepper and the orange juice. Then spread the Cornish Clotted Cream on and into this press the crab claw meat. Roll out the pastry and cover the pie dish, pressing the edges down to seal. Brush the pastry with the egg and bake at, 230°C/gas mark 8 for 25 mins.

Jed Rowe Aged 9,
Mevagissey Primary School

KIT HILL PIE

400g diced beef
½ swede
4 medium potatoes
1 onion
A little cornflour to thicken
2 beef stock cubes
Salt and pepper to taste

Shortcrust pastry
450g / 16oz self raising flour
225g / 8oz soft margarine
Pinch of salt
Skimmed milk

My mother was born on the side of Kit hill, in the village of Lucket, where she lived as a child with my Grandmother; this was always a favourite for my brother and I. The name comes from the stack on Kit Hill, as the pastry is either stacked on top, if you like it dry, or below the pie fill, if you prefer your pastry soaked in gravy. To this day my grandchildren ask for this dish whenever they visit, and it is still a favourite of mine.

Add the flour and margarine to a mixing bowl, and rub together until you get a breadcrumb like texture, add around half a cup of milk, and mix together, until the mix is all collected from the side of the bowl, not too wet or not too dry. Place the pastry in the refrigerator until you are ready to use. Cook this in a sauce pan on top the cooker. Stir the stock cubes into 600ml hot water, add the cubed beef and chopped onions, bring to the boil and simmer for 30 - 40 mins with a lid on. Add salt and pepper to taste. Large dice the swede, and add to the pan, simmer for a further 10 mins and then add the large diced potato. Top up the liquid to well cover the ingredients. Cook for a further 15 mins and at the same time, roll the pastry into a sheet, place on a tray and brush with egg. Bake in a moderate oven until golden. You can thicken the cook with a little corn flour in water, until its just as you like, re check for salt and pepper. You can either put the pasty on a plate and stack the fill onto it, or have the pastry on top of the mix, this is ideal served with fresh Cornish cabbage or carrots.

CHEESE AND BACON LOAF

225g / 8oz self raising flour
1 level tsp baking powder
2 level tsp mustard powder
50g / 2oz soft margarine
4 rashers of bacon (chopped)

1 large egg
100g / 4oz Cheddar cheese
140ml / ¼ pint milk
¼ level tsp salt and pepper

Grease a 2lb loaf tin. Place all the ingredients into a large mixing bowl, apart from 1oz of cheese which you will need later. Mix ingredients together thoroughly. Pour the mixture into the loaf tin. Sprinkle over the 1oz of cheese over the mixture.

Place in a pre-heated oven (190°C/375°F) and bake for 40 mins. Leave to cool in tin and serve the loaf sliced with butter.

Alex Pearce Aged 9,
Mevagissey Primary School

MINERS STEW

1ltr beef or lamb stock
Salt and pepper
500g leg of mutton chopped
(we used Lamb, worked perfectly)
150g chopped carrots
160g chopped parsnip
150g chopped swede

130g onions
250g chopped potatoes
60g chopped cabbage
Dumplings:
100g self raising flour
50g of suet
Cold water

Serves 4

This stew is a complete meal in itself. It does not need thickening but dumplings may be added if you wish. The Cornish housewife would adapt this recipe to the season. It is so tasty…

Bring the stock to the boil, season to taste, and add the meat. Simmer for 1 hour with the lid on. Add the carrots, parsnips, swede, onions and simmer for 15 mins. Add the potatoes and cabbage. Simmer until stew is well cooked and moist for approx. 15 mins, then add the dumplings and slow cook for a further 15 mins. Always keep the lid on as this helps cooking. Dumplings: Sift the flour into a mixing bowl. Mix in the suet, in to a good firm dough with water. Form into small balls and cook in boiling liquid for 20 mins.

Peter and Diane Jones, Queensland Australia, ex pats from the West Country, from an old Cornish recipe book. They found out about this book through the Ginsters friends and education Facebook page, and are firm admirers of the work of CHICKS.

Half the worlds tin came from Cornwall in the 1900s.

Fish Pie

1kg / 2.2lb potatoes
2 celery sticks
1 large onion
2 tbsp olive oil
150ml / 5fl oz double cream
50g / 2oz good strong cheddar cheese, grated
2 tsp fresh lemon juice
Small bunch parsley, finely chopped
400g / 14oz white fish, suggest haddock or cod
Salt and ground black pepper

Preparation time: 20 mins. Cooking time: 40 mins. Preheat the oven to gas mark 6/200°C. Wash and chop the potatoes and put in a large saucepan of cold, salted water. Bring to the boil and then simmer for about 12 - 15 mins or until soft. Once ready, drain the potatoes and put to one side. In the meantime, wash the celery and cut into small chunks. Peel and chop the onion. Warm the oil in a saucepan over a medium heat and gently sauté the celery and onion until the onion is softened, about 5 - 6 mins. Add the cream and cheese and stir just until the cheese has melted. Take off the heat and mix in the lemon juice and parsley. Cut the fish into bite-sized chunks, add to the vegetable/cream mixture and season to taste. Pour the mixture into an ovenproof dish. Mash the potatoes roughly with a little butter and milk and spread over the top, Put the pie in the oven and cook for 40 mins or until the potatoes are crisp and golden. Tip - sometimes in Cornwall we add cooked parsnip to the mash, and mash it together with the potato, which gives a really great taste.

The very first house to be gas lit in the world, was in Redruth in 1794.

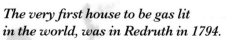

CORNISH YEAST CAKE

30g / 1oz yeast
50g / 2oz sugar
280ml / ½ pint tepid milk
450g / 1lb flour
Pinch of salt
50g / 2oz butter, softened
50g / 2oz lard
100g / 4oz currants and / or sultanas
50g / 2oz chopped mixed peel

Set oven to 200°C or mark 6. Grease a 7 inch cake tin or a baking sheet if making buns. Mix together the yeast and a teaspoon of the sugar, add the milk and set aside in a warm place to sponge. Sift the flour and salt into a bowl and rub in the fats until the mixture resembles breadcrumbs. Stir in the remaining sugar, the dried fruit and peel, then work in the yeast mixture and knead well. Return to the lightly greased or floured bowl and leave to rise in a warm place until doubled in size. Knock back, knead again and put into the tin or make into buns. Allow to prove in the warm for about 20 mins. When risen, bake the cake for about 30 mins or until a skewer inserted comes out clean or the buns for about 15 - 10 mins. Leave to cool and turn out on to a wire rack.

Ginsters employee

CORNISH FLATS

450g / 1lb flour
280ml / ½ pint Cornish cream
225g / 8oz caster sugar
1 egg, beaten
112g / 4oz sultanas or currants (optional)
Milk to mix

Set oven to 220°C or mark 7. Grease baking sheets. Put the cream into a bowl, sift in the flour add the sugar and beaten egg and mix with just sufficient milk to give a smooth, stiff dough. Roll out thinly on a lightly floured surface and cut into rounds with a 2 inch cutter. Put on the baking sheet and bake for about 10 mins until golden. Transfer to a wire rack and cool.

Ginsters employee

When an egg floats in water it is "off" and should not be eaten.

CORNISH HONEY FRUIT CAKE

86g / 3oz of caster sugar
113g / 4oz of margarine
2 large eggs
170g / 6oz of plain flour
113g / 4oz of Cornish honey
1 tsp of baking soda
2 tsp of mixed spice

454g / 1lb of mixed fruit (cherries, sultanas, raisins, etc.)
½ tsp of lemon juice
A pinch of salt
You will also require milk (use whole milk for best results)

In a large bowl mix the margarine, sugar and honey until smooth and creamy and sieve the flour, baking powder and mixed spice into the mixture. Add both eggs and beat the mixture well until the mixture is uniform and smooth. Now add the mixed fruit, lemon juice and a little bit of milk. Add a little milk at a time until you achieve a fairly soft and light consistency - be careful not to add too much. Put the mixture in a large cake tin lined with greased paper (use baking parchment and some extra margarine). We recommend a 7 inch square baking tin. Bake at 180°C for between 1 hour - 1 hour 15 mins. Place some baking parchment on top of the cake for the final 15 mins if the cake appears to be browning rapidly. Allow the cake to cool, and decorate or eat as it is with a nice cup of tea!

Bob McIntyre, Engineering Trainer for Ginsters

There is evidence that honey is the only food that cannot spoil. Archaeologists have tasted honey discovered in ancient Egyptian tombs, reporting that it's edible.

Cornish Sultana Cake

450g / 1lb flour
1 dstsp salt
170g / 6oz lard or butter
14g / 5oz fresh yeast
1 tsp caster sugar
425ml / ¾ pint tepid water
113g / 4oz sultanas
Chopped lemon peel (optional)

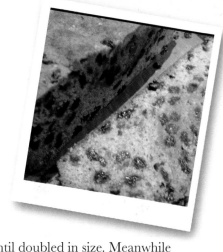

Grease a 2lb loaf tin. Sift the flour and salt into a bowl and rub in the fat until the mixture resembles breadcrumbs. Cream the yeast with the sugar and a little tepid water and add to the flour. Blend in sufficient of the remaining tepid water to mix to a soft dough that leaves the side of the bowl clean. Knead thoroughly on a floured surface, return to the lightly oiled or floured bowl, cover and leave to rise in a warm place until doubled in size. Meanwhile set oven to 400°F or mark 6. When risen, knock back and work in the currants and the lemon peel (if used). Put into the tin and leave in the warm to prove. Bake for about 1 to 1½ hours until brown on top and the bottom of the loaf sounds hollow when tapped. Transfer to wire rack to cool. Serve sliced and buttered.

Ginsters employee

Cornish Luncheon Cake

170g / 6oz butter, softened
170g / 6oz caster sugar
3 eggs
450g / 1lb self raising flour
1 tsp salt
1 teacup warm water and milk mixed
275g / 10oz sultanas
100g / 4oz chopped mixed peel
½ wine glass sweet sherry

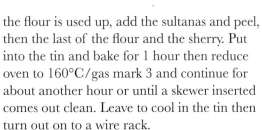

Set oven to 180°C or mark 5. Grease an 8 inch round cake tin. In a bowl, cream together the butter and sugar until light and fluffy. Add the eggs one at a time, beating to a creamy mixture. Sieve together the flour, and salt and gradually stir into the butter mixture alternatively with the milk/water, a little at a time. Just before all the flour is used up, add the sultanas and peel, then the last of the flour and the sherry. Put into the tin and bake for 1 hour then reduce oven to 160°C/gas mark 3 and continue for about another hour or until a skewer inserted comes out clean. Leave to cool in the tin then turn out on to a wire rack.

Ginsters employee

CORNISH STORE CAKE

225g / 8oz margarine
225g / 8oz caster sugar
4 eggs beaten
340g / 12oz flour
170g / 6oz currants
170g / 6oz sultanas
80g / 3oz glace cherries, quartered
80g / 3oz chopped mixed peel
50g / 2oz blanched almonds, chopped
Grated rind of 1 lemon

Set oven to 180°C or mark 4. Grease and line an 8 inch cake tin. In a bowl, cream together the margarine and sugar until light and fluffy. Beat in the eggs gradually, fold in the flour and add the dried fruit, glace cherries, peel, almonds and lemon rind. Put into the tin and back for 2½ hours or until a skewer inserted comes out clean. Leave to cool in the tin and turn out on to a wire rack.

Ginsters employee

CORNISH BURNT CREAM

850ml / 1 pint thick custard
570ml / 1 pint clotted cream
4 egg whites
Citron powder
Caster sugar

For this recipe you require two aluminium pudding basins, the smaller being able to fit inside the other and leave a ½ inch (12mm) gap all the way round. Put a layer of custard in the bottom of the smaller dish about 12mm thick, then a layer of clotted cream the same thickness, and repeat the layers until both custard and cream are fully used and ending with a cream layer. Sprinkle citron, or even thin lemon slices, on top then a dusting of caster sugar. Now whip the egg whites until stiff and place on the top. The smaller basin should now fit inside the larger and the gap packed with ice. Bake in a very hot oven about 260°C/gas mark 9, for 2½ mins or under a fierce grill to brown the top lightly.

Treve Nicol,
St Ives School

In 1842, near Redruth, the world's first elevator was demonstrated.

BLACKBERRY JAM

Having enjoyed the memories of picking blackberries during my childhood summer holidays I decided to relive that time. What a great day too, arms scratched to pieces, legs full of thorns, but well worth it.

My bounty was fresh juicy blackberries, and as I enjoyed my time in the kitchen, I found an old Cornish recipe from one of my mother's old books.

1.35kg / 3lb of blackberries
1.49kg / 3lb 5oz of jam sugar
½ lemon juice

2 eating apples (5oz)
Clean sterilised jars

First sort through the berries, and then wash them. Add half the lemon with the fruit to the pan, and bring to the boil. Peel and dice the 2 apples, very small, and add to the mix. Use a potato masher to help break up the fruit then add the rest of the lemon juice. Boil until the fruit is soft, and then add the sugar, stirring all the time. Bring to a fast boil. Boiling the mixture is very hot, so proceed with caution. The mix should bubble and rise up the pan. This needs to boil for around 10 mins, until set point is reached. Set point is checked the following way; before you start put two saucers into the freezer. After 10 mins of fast boiling, spoon a small amount onto one of the cold saucers, and place in fridge. Leave for a few minutes, and when you take it out check to see if a skin has formed and if you can push it with your finger. Once the point has been reached, remove from heat, and allow to cool for 10 mins, removing any scum from the top, and ladle into the jars. Seal the jars as soon as you can, preferably with a wax paper and band to keep it in place. Allow to cool and set, then keep in a cool place. It should store for three to four months.

Tradition says that you must not pick a blackberry after the 29th September, Michaelmass day, as that's when the devil spat on them, as it was bramble bushes that broke his fall from heaven, and he objected to the prickly thorns, so spat on them, and made them bitter!

In the South West of England it was believed that the first blackberry spotted growing each year would banish warts.

Countryside ways ask that you pick responsibly, always leave some for others, leave some for the wild life and do not pick more than you plan to use. There is always chance to go back again. Enjoy!

Chris Schaffer, Ginsters

The smaller the size of a berry, the sweeter its taste.

APPLE CHUTNEY

900g / 2lb cooking apples – peel and core
225g / 8oz onions – chopped
225g / 8oz raisins or sultanas
1 tsp salt
840g / 1½ pints distilled white malt vinegar
50g / 2oz mixed pickling spice
2 tsp ground ginger
450g / 1lb soft brown sugar

Put onions, apples, dried fruit, and salt in a pan with the
vinegar. Tie mixed pickling spice in muslin bag and add
to the pan. Bring to the boil and reduce heat and simmer
until tender. Remove spice bag and add ginger. Add sugar
and stir until dissolved. Continue to simmer until chutney
is thick, stirring occasionally to prevent sticking. Put into
hot clean jars, seal and label. Makes about 4lb.

Diane and Helen,
Cornwall Education Business Partnership

QUICK CUSTARD TART

Shortcrust pastry:
450g / 16oz self raising flour
225g / 8oz soft margarine
Pinch of salt
Skimmed milk
Filling:
3 eggs
2 tbsp caster sugar
112ml / ¼ pint milk
Nutmeg

Set the oven to 170°C/gas mark 4. To make
the shortcrust pastry, add the flour and
margarine to a mixing bowl, and rub together
until you get a breadcrumb like texture. Add
around half a cup of milk, and mix together
until the mix is all collected from the side of
the bowl, not too wet or not too dry. Place the
pastry in the refrigerator until you are ready to
use. Then line a tart plate with the shortcrust
pastry. Whisk eggs in a basin, add caster sugar
and milk, and mix well. Pour into pastry case,
sprinkle with nutmeg and bake until set for
about 20 mins. Using muffin cases will give
you individual tarts.

Diane and Helen, Cornwall EBP

The worlds first steam engine was built in Camborne, by Richard Trevithick in 1801.

GRANNY ROSE'S CHOCOLATE CAKE

175g soft margarine
175g caster sugar
175g self raising flour
50g cocoa powder
3 medium eggs
100g / 4oz butter
225g / 8oz icing sugar

Cream margarine and sugar together and mix together. Then add the cocoa powder. Beat the eggs and add to mixture then add the flour and mix together. After that put into 2 sponge cake tins. Cook at 180°C for up to 20 - 25 mins. The take the cake out to cool, and fill with butter cream icing. Make this by placing the softened butter in a mixing bowl and sift the icing sugar over the top. Add the flavouring of your choice (optional) and cream all the ingredients together with a wooden spoon until well blended. You can add melted chocolate to the top if you would prefer as well.

**Elizabeth Trevarton Aged 9,
Mevagissey School**

CORNISH FAIRINGS

112g / 4oz butter
112g / 4oz sugar
225g / 8oz flour
4 tbsp golden syrup
½ tsp salt
2 tsp baking powder

2 tsp bicarbonate of soda
2 tsp mixed spice
3 tsp ground ginger
1 tsp cinnamon

Sieve together the flour, salt, spices and baking powder and bicarbonate of soda. Rub in the butter and add the sugar. Spoon the syrup in to a cup, stand in shallow water in a pan and heat gently until soft. Pour the liquid syrup onto the other ingredients and work in thoroughly. With floury hands roll the mixture into small balls and place on a greased baking tray, well spaced out. Bake at 200°C, 15 - 20 mins, moving the biscuits from the top to the bottom shelf of the oven the moment they begin to brown. If the centre is not crispy it will harden once they are removed from the oven.

**Kirby Boothroyd,
St Ives School**

Cornish Bread and Butter Pudding

8 slices of stale bread (crusts as well), any type
425ml / ¾ pint milk (we use Trewithen full cream milk)
2 eggs (preferably Cornish free range eggs)
Nutmeg to taste
Cornish butter
225g / 8oz dried fruit
112g / 4oz sugar

Butter the bread and cut into triangles. You can butter both sides of the bread if you would prefer. Grease a deep sided cake tin, and add a layer of buttered bread. Sprinkle with sugar and dried fruit. Repeat layers until all the bread is evenly distributed, then mix the egg and milk and pour over the bread.

Press down firmly to compress the pudding and help the bread absorb the milk mixture. Pop in the oven at 180°C/gas mark 4 and bake until golden brown and the custard mixture is set. Can be accompanied by custard, cream or ice cream (all should be Cornish!).

Bill Clark, Trewithen Dairies

Cornish Banana Cake

For the cake:
225g / 8oz very ripe banana (weight after peeling)
90g / 3½ oz caster sugar
90g / 3½ oz butter, softened
200g / 7oz self raising flour, sifted
1 egg, beaten
½ tsp bicarbonate of soda
1 tbsp milk

For the filling:
1 ripe banana
50g / 2oz butter, softened
50g / 2oz caster sugar

For the icing:
1 soft, very ripe banana
25g / 1oz cocoa powder, sifted
225g / 8oz icing sugar, sifted

Pre-heat the oven to 180°C/350°F. Butter two 7 inch round sandwich tins and lightly flour, tapping any excess out. Mash the bananas and sugar together for the cake in a bowl with an electric mixer. Beat in the softened butter. Add the flour alternately with the egg. Dissolve the soda in the milk and add to the mixture. Beat to a fairly sticky batter. Divide evenly between the two tins, smooth the tops and then bake for 35 - 40 mins until the sponge springs back when lightly touched. Remove from the oven and turn out onto a wire rack to cool completely. To make the filling, beat all the ingredients together until well mixed and use to sandwich the two layers together. For the icing, beat all the ingredients together until dark and really smooth. Spread onto the top of the cake. Note - if you like you can decorate the top with some blanched almonds, walnut halves or dried banana chips.

Katie Pimlott, Learning and Development Assistant, Ginsters

Banana trees are not actually trees – they are giant herbs.

Cornwall Cakes are based in Bude, North Cornwall and have been making award-winning desserts for over a decade. Their small team of chefs produce hand-made cakes and desserts, sourcing their ingredients locally where possible in order showcase the great products available and to achieve the best possible taste. Their main business is supplying hotels, restaurants and tea-shops across the South West. They are happy to supply to individuals for private events and parties. They also offer personalised celebrations cakes tailored to your specification. Call 01288 356861 or visit www.cornwallcakes.co.uk for more information. In the meantime why not try making our Cornish fruit cake, delicious anytime of the day!

CORNISH FRUIT CAKE

225g sultanas
225g currants
115g demerara
150ml hot tea (1 bag)
50g eggs
15ml water
225g self raising flour, sifted

Makes 1 2lb loaf. Dissolve sugar in hot tea and then pour over sultanas and currants. Cover and leave to soak overnight. Beat eggs and add this and the water to the mix. Gradually combine flour. Spoon into loaf tin lined with greaseproof paper, or loaf liner. Bake at 150°C for 1 hour 30 mins approx. Serve sliced and spread thick with butter.

Ben Dayman
Cornwall Cakes Ltd.

In 1901, the first transatlantic radio message was sent from the Lizard to its inventor, Marconi in Newfoundland.

Rodda's Cornish Whoopie Pies

100g butter, softened
185g unrefined light muscovado sugar
1 egg
35g cocoa
300g plain flour
1 tsp bicarbonate of soda
1 tsp baking powder
A pinch of salt
1 tsp vanilla extract
100 - 125ml milk
227g Rodda's Cornish Clotted Cream

Preparation Time: 10 mins. Cooking Time: 15 mins. Makes: 20 - 30 halves (so that's 10 - 15 filled Whoopies). Preheat fan oven to 180°C/fan oven 160°C /300°F/gas mark 3. Lightly grease baking sheets. In a large bowl, cream together the butter, sugar, and egg. In another bowl, sieve and combine cocoa, flour, bicarbonate of soda, baking powder, and salt. In a small bowl, stir the vanilla extract into the milk. Add the dry ingredients to the butter mix, alternating with the milk mixture; beating until smooth. Drop batter using two spoons (to make 20 - 30 halves or 10 - 15 Whoopies when filled with cream) onto the prepared baking sheets. With the back of a spoon spread batter into 5cm/2 inch circles, leaving approximately 4cm/2 inch between each cake. Bake for 15 mins or until they are firm to the touch. Remove from oven and let cool completely on a wire rack. When the cakes are completely cool, spread the flat side (bottom) of one chocolate cake with a generous amount of Rodda's Cornish Clotted Cream. Top with another cake, pressing down gently to distribute the filling evenly. Repeat to make 10 - 15 whoopies. Decorate in your own individual style.

Rodda's

Thunder and Lightning

A simple recipe for a quick treat:
Take one slice of bread and spread it with golden syrup. Then on top mix in clotted cream, for extra sweetness sprinkle some brown sugar on top. This is an old Cornish Recipe and not for anyone who is calorie conscious.

Ginsters employee

CORNISH SPLITS (SPLYTYS KERNEWEK)

140ml / ¼ pint milk
25g / 1oz yeast
½ tsp sugar
140ml / ¼ pint warm water
680g / 1½ lb flour
110g / 4oz butter
25g / 1oz lard

Put the sugar, yeast and 1 teaspoon of flour in a basin, mix well with warm water and leave in a warm place for 15 mins. Sieve the flour into a basin and leave. Gently heat the milk, add the lard and butter, allow it to blend together. Make a well in the middle of the flour and gradually pour in the yeast water and the warmed milk, and butter and lard, mixing all into soft dough. Leave for around 1 ½ hours to rise. Knead for 4 mins on a floured surface; roll out ½ inch (12mm) thick. Cut into pieces and form into small balls about the size and shape of a tangerine. Bake for 20 - 30 mins until golden brown. Once cold split in half; fill with your favourite jam, and a generous portion of clotted cream.

Stephanie Hamilton-Jones, St Ives School

CREAMED APPLES

½ dozen apples
½ cupful Cornish Clotted Cream
1 tbsp lemon juice
3 tbsp caster sugar
2 tbsp Cornish strawberry jam
(or any other flavour you fancy)

Bake the apples until soft and scoop out the insides then pass them through a sieve. Put into a bowl, add the Cornish Clotted Cream and lemon juice. Beat in the caster sugar. Fill the apples with this mix. Serve chilled and place the strawberry jam on top in the middle just before you serve.

Luke Wheeler Aged 9, Mevagissey Primary School

CORNISH HEAVY CAKE

350g / 12oz plain flour
2.4ml / ½ tsp salt
175g / 6oz lard (shortening)
75g / 3oz caster sugar
175g / 6oz currants
A little chopped mixed (candied) peel (optional)
About 150ml mixed milk and water
1 beaten egg
Chopped lemon peel (optional)

Place the flour and salt in a bowl, then rub in the lard until the mixture resembles breadcrumbs. Stir in the remaining dry ingredients. Gradually add enough milk and water to make a stiff dough; it will not take very much. Roll out on to a greased baking (cookie) sheet to about 1cm/½ inch thick. Glaze with beaten egg. Bake in a pre-heated oven at 160°C/325°F/gas mark 3 for about 20 mins until golden. Allow to cool, then cut into squares.

Katie Perry and Jordan Bromley,
St Ives School A Technology College

CORNISH JUNKET

1 pint full fat milk
Sugar
Essence of rennet and nutmeg

Heat 1 pint of full fat milk to body temperature (so it's luke warm). As it is warming up add 1 tablespoon of sugar to sweeten it up, do not overheat the milk. Once warmed, remove the heat. Add 2 teaspoons of essence of rennet and stir into milk then pour it into the amount of dishes you want. Next sprinkle grated nutmeg on top of the puddings and place somewhere cool to set.

Susanna James, Mevagissey School

CORNISH APPLE PIE

Pastry:
200g / 7oz all purpose, plain flour
1 tbsp sugar
110g / 1 stick butter,
cubed or an equal mix of butter and margarine
2 - 3 tbsp cold water
Filling:
700g / 1½lbs cooking apples,
peeled, cored and quartered
100g / ½ cup sugar
4 - 6 tbsp cold water
1 level tsp ground cinnamon
2 tbsp lemon juice
25g / ¼ stick butter
Egg to glaze

Place the flour, butter and sugar into a large clean bowl. Rub the butter into the flour with your fingertips until the mixture resembles fine breadcrumbs, working as quickly as possible to prevent the dough becoming warm. Add the water to the mixture and using a cold knife stir until the dough binds together, add more cold water a teaspoons at a time if the mixture is too dry. Wrap the dough in cling film and chill for a minimum of 15 mins, up to 30 mins. The dough can also be made in a food processor by mixing the flour, butter and salt in a bowl of the processor on a pulse setting. When the mixture resembles breadcrumbs, add the water, slowly, through the funnel until the dough comes together in a call. Wrap in clingfilm and chill as above. Heat the oven to 425°F/220°C/gas mark 7.

Meanwhile simmer the apples with the water in a large pan until soft. Add the sugar and cinnamon to the cooked apples. Remove from the heat and add the butter and leave to cool. Roll out half the pastry and line a 7 inch/13cm pie dish. Put the cooled, cooked apple mixture to the pastry case. Roll out the remaining pastry to make a lid for the pie. Damp the edges of the pastry in the dish with a little cold water, cover with the lid and press the edges firmly together and crimp the edges to decorate. Brush the top of the pie with egg, sprinkle with sugar and bake at the top of a hot oven for 20 - 25 mins. Serve hot or cold with Cornish Clotted Cream, ice cream or custard sauce.

Eilish Saunders,
St Ives School

Cornwall's greatest legend must be King Arthur, said to have been born in Tintagel.

CORNISH SAFFRON CAKE WITH CLOTTED CREAM

½ tsp saffron strands
½ cup milk and water combined
500g unbleached white bread flour
1 tsp fine sea salt
150g butter or fat (cut into small chunks)
50g light muscovado sugar
15g fresh yeast
100g mixed fruit

Boil half a cup of the milk and water mix. Cut the saffron into very fine strands with scissors. Place in a glass jug and pour the boiling milk and water over it. Cover and leave over night. Preheat oven to 180°C/350°F/gas mark 4 and grease a suitable-sized loaf tin for your saffron cake. Put the fresh yeast into a small bowl with a teaspoon of the muscovado sugar and half a cup of luke warm milk and water combined (if it is too hot it will kill the yeast). Rub the butter or fat into the flour until the mixture resembles breadcrumbs, stir in the rest of the sugar (not the yeast and sugar mixture). When yeast has risen in the small bowl, make a pit in the centre of the flour mixture and pour in the yeast, covering with a sprinkle of flour. When this mixture cracks and the yeast 'sponges' through, warm the previously made saffron mixture a little and add this to the mix, together with the mixed fruit. Combine using your hand to make a soft (but not sticky)

dough (add a little more water at this stage if required). Knead the dough for 5 mins on a floured surface. Cover with a clean towel and leave in a warm place to rise for about 30 - 45 mins. Put into a greased loaf tin, cover and leave to rise again until it is level with the top of the tin for about 60 mins. Bake for 45 - 60 mins. Leave to cool on a wire rack.

Clotted Cream Instructions:
Pour milk into a basin or dish, and leave in a cool place for at least 8 hours. The cream will rise to the top. Put the dish over a pot of boiling water, you may want to use a double boiler. Simmer the water until the cream begins to show a ring around the edge and the surface just begins to bubble. After about 45 mins to an hour, remove from heat. Let the cream cool and skim the clotted cream from the surface.

Ashleigh Jukes, St Ives School

Saffron, made from the dried stamens of cultivated crocus flowers, is the most expensive cooking spice.

FIGGIE HOBBIN

2 cups self raising flour
1 tsp suet
1 tsp lard
Figs or raisins
Cold milk or water to mix

Rub the lard and suet into the flour. Add the figs or raisins and mix to a stiff dough with a little milk or water. Roll out to a thickness of ½ inch and cut into 4 inch squares. Make a slash across the top of each with a knife and bake in a moderate oven for about 30 mins.

Rory James Dixon, Aged 10,
Jack Hocking, Aged 10 and Flyn Lakeman
Aged 9, Mevagissey School

CORNISH SWEETHEART TART

170g / 6oz shortcrust pastry
170g / 6oz caster sugar
170g / 6oz butter, melted
110g / 4oz dried apricots
50g / 2oz roasted hazelnuts
2 eggs
Breadcrumbs to scatter on top

Pre-heat oven to 180°C/350°F/gas mark 4. Chop the apricots and hazelnuts. Beat the eggs and yolks with the sugar, add the melted butter. Line a 25cm (10 inch) baking tin with the pastry scatter then with the apricots and hazelnuts. Pour in the egg mixture, sprinkle with breadcrumbs and bake for 30 - 40 mins, until the crust is a rich, golden brown. Serve warm and with clotted cream.

 Daisy Hatton, St Ives School

APPLE AND BEETROOT CAKE

50g butter
200g soft brown sugar
200g self raising flour
5g baking powder
100ml sunflower oil
2 eggs
300g grated beetroot
75g diced apple

75g toasted walnuts
Zest of one orange
Syrup:
220ml water
150g caster sugar
Juice of half a lemon

Heat the butter in a small pan until it browns and smells nutty. Add the sunflower oil and leave to cool. Whisk the eggs and sugar until pale and thick. Gradually pour in the oil and butter mixture as if you're making mayonnaise. Sift the flour and baking powder over the egg mixture and fold in. Add the remaining ingredients, beetroot, apple, walnuts and zest. Mix well, then transfer to a greased and lined tin. Bake at 180°C for 40 mins - 1 hour (until a skewer comes out clean). To make the syrup, heat all of the ingredients in a pan until the sugar dissolves. Prick the cake all over with a fork and douse with the syrup.

Duchy College, Stoke Climsland

CALLINGTON BUNS

500g self raising flour
Cinnamon (optional)
250g margarine
3 eggs beaten
185g sugar
60g candied lemon peel
125g mixed dried fruits
Lemon essence
Milk

Sift the flour and cinnamon twice. Rub in the margarine, and then add the eggs beating well until smooth. Add the sugar, lemon peel, and dried fruits. Mix the lemon essence and enough milk to form a stiff consistency. Place in small heaps on a greased oven tray and brush with milk. Bake in a hot oven for 20 mins.

Peter and Diane Jones, QLD Australia

Callington was once a market town, and it sits on the side of Kit Hill, and the glorious Tamar Valley. Today it is also known as the home of Ginsters, where the family business started in 1967.

GRISSINI

500g strong white bread flour, sifted
1 tsp salt
2 tsp dried yeast
3 tbsp olive oil
275ml warm water
A little beaten egg to glaze
Salt crystals
Semolina for rolling out
Makes 40

These tasty breadsticks are easy to make and provide the perfect accompaniment to a nicely chilled glass of Camel Valley 'Cornwall' sparkling wine. Originally from Turin, this is our own recipe for the grissini we serve at our wine tastings, and they are always very popular for pre-dinner drinks as they don't curb the appetite. Place 125ml of the water in a food processor, sprinkle on the yeast and stir to dissolve. Leave for about 10 mins till frothy. Add the flour, salt and olive oil and the rest of the water, and mix on pulse several times till well mixed, smooth and elastic. Leave with the lid on in a warm place for an hour or two till well risen. Heat the oven to 200°C/400°F. We cook ours on the lowest set of runners in the Aga, turning after 5 mins. Mix again then turn the dough out on to a worktop sprinkled with semolina. Divide into 4 portions, and roll each one out into a rectangle about 12cm wide by 25cm, using a little more semolina on top. Brush with beaten egg then sprinkle with a few salt crystals and roll lightly so they stick to the dough. Cut into 10 strips with a sharp knife and place about 1cm apart on a silicone baking sheet. Leave in a warm place while you prepare the other portions in the same way. By now the first batch should have risen a little. Bake for 15 mins and cool on a wire rack. Irresistible when warm, they will keep for a few days in a tin, or can be frozen when cold. Remember, you're wasting your time without a glass of Camel Valley to go with them!

Bob Lindo

CORNISH FRUIT MOLD

8 slices of bread
750g blackberries
750g blackcurrants
750g redcurrants
750g raspberries
750g strawberries or loganberries
Sugar
Ensure fruit juice is allowed to soak into the bread

Line a greased pudding basin with slices of bread. Fill the basin with alternate layers of berry fruits and slices of bread, sprinkle each layer liberally with sugar, and ending with bread. Cover with a plate and put a heavy weight on top. Leave in the refrigerator overnight to set. Remove from the mold and serve with Cornish Clotted Cream. Serves 6.

CORNISH MEAD

1.36kg / 3lbs clear honey
4.55ltr / 1 gallon water
2 lemons
56g / 2oz root ginger
28g / 1oz yeast
Rosemary sprig

This drink was traditionally drunk by newly wed couples for a month after the wedding hence the term "honeymoon". The water should be boiled for 30 mins then the honey stirred in and the mixture simmered for a further hour. Remove any scum produced with a wooden spoon. The ginger should first be bruised and tied in a muslin bag along with the rosemary. This is added to the fluid along with the juice and the rind of the lemons.

When cooled to luke warm add the yeast and stir. Cover the vessel and stand in a warm place removing the muslin bag and floating lemon peel after 5 days but allow the mixture to ferment for a further 6 days. Strain with a cloth sieve and bottle, leaving the corks loose initially but when the gas production ceases tighten home. It should be kept bottled for at least two months before drinking.

Andrew Morris, Product Development Manager, Tamar Foods

SIMPLY THE BEST ICE CREAM SUNDAE OR BOMBE

Here at Callestick Farm, we take our own pure, wholesome milk, local cream and the finest fruits and confectionery. Then we add a touch of Callestick magic to create flavour upon flavour of dreamy, ice creamy indulgence.

The farm has been run by us (the Parker family) for many generations and we have been making our award-winning ice cream for 20 years. Our ice cream is completely natural; none of the rich dairy goodness is removed and nothing artificial is added...Fresh natural and utterly indulgent. Made with Callestick Farm's Clotted Cream Vanilla ice cream and their Belgian Chocolate ice cream... with brownies, cream and chocolate sauce... yum yum! It's so easy... take squares of your favourite Brownie recipe and add to a wide mouthed ice cream sundae glass or deep bowl. Scoop on top first a large vanilla ball of ice cream and then

a rich chocolate scoop - cover with a dollop of Cornish Clotted Cream and some warm homemade chocolate sauce. These can be prepared just before eating or they can be scooped in advance, to the cream and chocolate sauce stage and put back into the freezer until you are ready. Then simply pull out, decorate and serve! Alternatively to make the bombe - gently mix all ingredients, ice creams and brownies in a pudding basin so that it is full to the top. Cover with cling film and freeze fast. When ready to serve dip the bowl in warm water to loosen the ice cream and invert onto a chilled plate. Drizzle chocolate sauce over the bombe and decorate the top with chocolate flake or if you prefer dark chocolate shavings. Just watch the delight on friends and families' faces when you produce these! The secret is to always use the very best ingredients.

Here's a sauce recipe I have used successfully:

Use 150ml / 6oz best dark chocolate, 50g / 2oz butter,
4 tbsp / 60ml water, 50g / 2oz caster sugar

Make the chocolate sauce by putting all the ingredients together in a pan and heating gently stirring all the time. Allow to cool and thicken and pour over your prepared bombe or sundae.

Callestick Far
Cornish Dairy Ice Cr

NEWQUAY PUDDING

125g fresh breadcrumbs
3 eggs, separated
2 tbsp sugar
625ml milk
Raspberry jam to spread
Desiccated coconut
50g / 2oz caster sugar for the milk mix
6 tbsp caster sugar for the meringue top

Put the breadcrumbs in a greased pie-dish. Beat the egg-yolk, add the sugar and milk, then pour over the crumbs. Leave to stand for half an hour. Bake in a warm oven for about an hour, or until set. Do not allow to boil. Remove from the oven, spread liberally with raspberry jam, and lightly sprinkle with coconut. Beat the egg-whites until stiff, add 3 tablespoons caster sugar, and beat again. Fold in the last 3 tablespoons of caster sugar to make the meringue. Pile on the pudding and form small peaks, and return to the oven until golden. Serve with clotted cream. Serves 6.

From Peter and Diane Jones, Queensland, Australia

CORNISH CREAM TEA

1lb self raising flour
3oz margarine
2oz granulated sugar
2 large eggs
½ pint of milk
4oz sultanas

Place flour and margarine into a mixing bowl. Use fingers to mix the two into a crumble, and then add other dry ingredients. Place 2 eggs into a jug and whisk gently and add milk to bring up to half a pint. Pour into dry mixture, leaving a little for glazing. Using hands mix into a dough, until the mixture comes away from the bowl. On a flour dusted surface pat out until dough is roughly 1½ inches in height. Cut out using a round cutter. Place on pre-greased and floured tray allowing room to rise. Using remaining egg mixture, glaze top evenly. Place into the centre of a pre-heated oven gas mark 7. Allow to bake for 10 - 15 mins. Wait for them to cool and serve with your favourite jam (traditionally strawberry) and serve with a hefty spoonful of Cornish Clotted Cream. Eat and enjoy!!!

When we visit our grandparents in Cornwall, Nan always has to make these for us, as we love them - Bryony, Lauren and Thomas McNally, now living in Derbyshire.

Halwin School is a small primary school located 4 miles from the town of Helston. The school is mainly a Victorian building with a large, modern hall extension.

The school achieved a Healthy School status in June 2003 and again in 2005 and 2007. The children are encouraged to eat healthily. Cookery is a firm favourite with the pupils and there is always a waiting list for Cookery Club.

PENZANCE CAKE

450g / 1lb flour
450g / 1lb currants
14g / ½oz ginger
112g / 4oz peel
112g / 4oz butter
14g / ½oz ground cinnamon
2 eggs
1 tsp baking-soda to be dissolved in a cup of warm milk

Cream the butter in the flour and mix in the dry ingredients. Beat the eggs well and stir in with wooden spoon, then the milk. Add this to a baking tin, bake for 2½ - 3 hours in a slow oven.

Halwin School, Porkellis, Helston

HELSTON PUDDING

50g / 2oz each of raisins, currants, suet, sugar and breadcrumbs
Ground rice and small piece candied peel
½ tsp bicarbonate soda
½ tsp mixed spice
50g / 2oz flour
Little salt and milk

Clean fruit and cut peel finely. Dissolve soda in milk, mix together all dry ingredients and add milk. Pour all into a well-greased basin, cover with greased paper and stand in a saucepan of boiling water and boil for 2 hours.

Halwin School, Porkellis, Helston

Legend says that the Devil was carrying a stone back to gates of hell when St Michael fought with him. The stone was dropped, and where it fell became known as Hells Town; hence the name Helston.

Our pure, brilliantly white, flaky sea salt crystals melt in the mouth and add real flavour intensity to the foods you like to eat.

With Soil Association accreditation it retains over sixty naturally occurring trace elements essential for well-being; Cornish Sea Salt delivers more taste for less salt, making it a tastier and healthier alternative to traditional table salt.

We have been making significant waves in the culinary world, with some of the UK's leading chefs on board and gaining a 'Good Food Award' gold star this year – the tide is turning towards Cornish Sea Salt.

CORNISH SEA SALT™ ROAST POTATOES

2½kg floury potatoes
(preferably Desiree, King Edward or Romano)
½ tsp turmeric
2 x 320g jars goose fat
½ tsp paprika
Cornish Sea Salt™ Original

Serves 10

Preheat oven to 190°C/gas mark 5/fan 170°C. Peel the potatoes and cut into big chunks. Put them in a large saucepan of boiling salted water, sprinkle in the turmeric and give a good stir. Bring back to the boil, then cover and simmer the potatoes for about 8 mins. Drain the potatoes and place in a cold, open tray or dish to cool completely. Scratch roughly with a fork (the rougher surface will give you crispier potatoes). Season well with Cornish Sea Salt (simply crumble the crystals between your fingers as you go – no need to shake or grind!). Heat the goose fat in the roasting tin until it is sizzling hot and then tip the potatoes into the hot fat. Baste or turn the potatoes (carefully) as soon as they go into the roasting tin so they have a light coating of goose fat from the start. Scatter with a light sprinkling of paprika and roast for 1¼ hours or until golden and crisp. Baste (or turn) at least once. To serve, sprinkle the potatoes with Cornish Sea Salt and freshly ground black pepper and serve immediately.

Time to convert, here is some information to help you:

GAS MARK	°C	DESCRIPTION
a quarter	110	Very Slow
half	130	Very Slow
1	140	Very Slow
2	150	Slow
3	160	Slow
4	180	Very Moderate
5	190	Moderate
6	200	Moderately Hot
7	220	Moderately Hot
8	230	Hot

OUNCES	GRAMS
¼ (quarter)	7
½ (half)	14
¾ (three quarters)	21
1	28.35
2	57
3	85
4 (¼ lb.)	113
5	142
6	170
7	198
8 (½ lb.)	227
9	255 (¼ kilo)
10	284
11	312
12 (¾ lb)	340
13	369
14	397
15	425
16 (1 lb.)	454

ACKNOWLEDGEMENTS

Ginsters would like to thank the following for their contributions to this book

St Ives School, Cornwall

Mevagissey School, Cornwall

Halwin School, Cornwall

Andrew, Andy and Tracy at Brewers, part of the Martin Luck group

Major International

Dairy Crest and Davidstow Cheddar

Rodda's Cornish Cream

Cornwall Cakes

Skinners Brewery

Trewithan Dairy

St Austell Brewery

Cornish Orchards

Callestick Ice Cream

Camel Valley Wines

Cornish Blue Cheese Co.

Cornish Sea Salt

The Ginsters Camera Club

Jenny Patton and staff at CHICKS

Shelley Clowes for all her cooking

Victoria Lyth

Emily Rixon

Dee Schaffer

Katie Pimlott

Chris Bettinson

Diane Capper

Design donated by Bluestone360